I Love You
You
Dad

C O U P O N S

Sourcebooks, Inc.
Naperville, IL

Published by Sourcebooks Inc., P.O. Box 372, Naperville, IL 60566 (630) 961-3900 FAX: (630) 961-2168

Internal design and production by Andrew Sardina and Scott Theisen

Printed and bound in the United States of America.
10 9 8 7 6 5 4 3

Sourcebooks would like to thank the following individuals for sharing their fun and creative coupon ideas…

Cassie, CA
Santos, CA
Josselyn, CA
Nessia, NY
Gen, NM
Tiffany, TX
Rebecca, OH
Johanna, FL

I Love
You
Dad

COUPONS

THIS COUPON
ENTITLES DAD
TO ONE WEEK OF
BACK RUBS
EVERY NIGHT

Personal notes _____

_____

"*For reasons I can't explain, I really like being a parent. It's just there's a lot more to it than I expected.*"

—Dave Barry

I Love
You
Dad

C O U P O N S

DAD, BECAUSE I LOVE YOU,
I WILL LET YOU WIN THE
NEXT ONE-ON-ONE
BASKETBALL GAME

Personal notes _____

_____

"I don't want to be a pal,
I want to be a father."

—Clifton Fadiman

I Love You
You
Dad

This coupon entitles Dad to quiet while he is on the phone

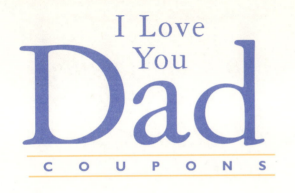

Personal notes _____

_____

"Don't take up a man's time talking about the smartness of your children; he wants to talk to you about the smartness of his children."

—Ed Howe

I Love You
You
Dad
C O U P O N S

Dad, because I love you, I will go to bed without complaining

Personal notes _____

_____

"*The child is father of the man.*"

—William Wordsworth

I Love You

You

Dad

C O U P O N S

This coupon is good for hugs and kisses

Personal notes _____

_____

"If you give your life as a wholehearted response to love, then love will wholeheartedly respond to you."

—Marianne Williamson

I Love You
Dad
C O U P O N S

DAD, BECAUSE I LOVE YOU, I WILL RAKE THE YARD, WATER THE PLANTS, AND SWEEP THE DECK FOR A WEEK

Personal notes _____

_____

"Children are a poor men's riches."

—English proverb

I Love You

You

Dad

C O U P O N S

This coupon entitles Dad to control of the TV remote for an evening

Personal notes _____

_____

"We never know the love of the parent till we become parents ourselves."

—Henry Ward Beecher

I Love
You

Dad

C O U P O N S

DAD, BECAUSE I
LOVE YOU, I
WILL SHOVEL
THE SNOW

Personal notes _____

_____

"Our father...had cast a magic over everything, for us as well as for her. He held his love up over us like an umbrella and kept off the troubles that afterward came down on us."

—Mary Lavin

I Love You

You

Dad

C O U P O N S

THIS COUPON ENTITLES
DAD TO AN ENTIRE DAY
FREE OF WHINING

Personal notes _____

_____

"Happy [is] that man whose children make his happiness in life and not his grief."

—Euripedes

I Love You
Dad
C O U P O N S

INSTANT COUPON!

Clean your room!

Personal notes _____

_____

"Honor thy father and thy mother."

—Exodus 20:12

I Love
You
Dad

C O U P O N S

This coupon entitles
Dad to a shopping
trip to the store of
his choice

Personal notes _____

_____

"A man travels the world over in search of what he needs and returns home to find it."

—George Moore

I Love
You
Dad
C O U P O N S

ÏNSTANT COUPON!

Get off the Internet!

Personal notes _____

_____

"He that will have his son have respect for him and his orders, must himself have a great reverence for his son."

—John Locke

I Love You

You

Dad

C O U P O N S

This coupon entitles
Dad to sleep in late on
the day of his choice

Personal notes _____

_____

"Parents have a job that requires lots of experience to perform and none at all to get."

—Unknown

I Love
You
Dad

C O U P O N S

DAD, BECAUSE I LOVE YOU,
I WILL HELP YOU PAINT
THE DECK/FENCE/SHED

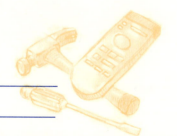

Personal notes _____

_____

"You are the bows from which your children are as living arrows sent forth."

—Kahlil Gibran

I Love You

Dad

C O U P O N S

THIS COUPON ENTITLES DAD TO A NIGHT OUT ON THE TOWN

Personal notes _____

_____

"There is no more vital calling or vocation for men than fathering."

—John R. Throop

I Love
You
Dad
C O U P O N S

No TV at Dinner Coupon.
This coupon entitles Dad
to a family dinner free
of interruption

Personal notes _____

_____

"He knows, without doubt, that in wife and child he has the only treasures that really matter anyway."

—Lewis Grizzard

I Love You Dad

COUPONS

This coupon is good
for breakfast in bed
one Sunday

Personal notes _____

_____

"It doesn't matter who my father was;
it matters who I remember he was."

—Anne Sexton

I Love
You
Dad

**Dad, because
I love you,
I will make
my bed for a
week without
being told**

Personal notes _____

_____

"*...what my father used to say*
Is good enough for me."

—A.P. Herbert

I Love
You
Dad

C O U P O N S

THE WILD CARD COUPON.
THIS COUPON
ENTITLES DAD TO

_____

_____

Personal notes _____

_____

"The debt of gratitude we owe our mother and father goes forward, not backward. What we owe our parents is the bill presented to us by our children."

—Nancy Friday

I Love
You
Dad

C O U P O N S

FREE WEEKEND!

This weekend, Dad
has no chores
or responsibilities

Personal notes _____

_____

"As soon as you become a father, your job is cut out for you. It is probably the most significant job you will ever have."

—Paul Heidebrecht

I Love You
You
Dad

C O U P O N S

Dad, because I love you, I will be ready to leave for

_____ **early**

Personal notes _____

_____

"The quality of a child's relationship with his or her father seems to be the most important influence in deciding how that person will react to the world."

—John Nicholson

I Love
You
Dad

C O U P O N S

Personal notes _____

_____

Dad Wins the Argument Coupon. Stop arguing! With this coupon, Dad automatically wins!

"When I was a boy of fourteen, my father was so ignorant I could hardly stand to have the old man around. But when I got to be twenty-one, I was astounded at how much he had learned in seven years."

—Mark Twain

I Love You
Dad
C O U P O N S

DAD, BECAUSE I LOVE YOU, I WILL TAKE OUT THE GARBAGE

Personal notes _____

_____

"*Every father expects his boy to do the things he wouldn't do when he was young.*"

—Kin Hubbard

I Love You
You
Dad
C O U P O N S

Personal notes _____

_____

Kids stop fighting!

"*The most important thing a father can do for his children is to love their mother.*"

—Theodore M. Hesburgh

I Love You
You
Dad

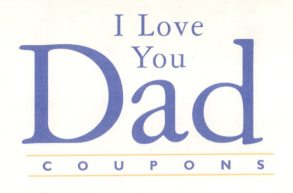

C O U P O N S

Dad, because I love you, I will wash the car

Personal notes _____

_____

"*The great man is he who dares not lose his child's heart.*"

—Mencius

I Love
You

Dad

C O U P O N S

SPORTS-FEST SUNDAY
COUPON! THIS
COUPON IS GOOD
FOR ONE SUNDAY OF
UNINTERRUPTED TIME
TO WATCH THE SPORT
OF DAD'S CHOICE

Personal notes _____

_____

"The father is the head of a unit of people launched on an exploration of life and all the things God has placed in the world for us to discover and enjoy."

—Gordon MacDonald

I Love You
You
Dad

DAD, BECAUSE I LOVE YOU, I WILL PULL THE WEEDS IN THE YARD

Personal notes _____

_____

"A man's children and his garden both reflect the amount of weeding done during the growing season."

—Unknown

I Love You
Dad
C O U P O N S

This coupon entitles
Dad to read the
evening paper
without interruption

Personal notes _____

_____

"How many hopes and fears, how many ardent wishes and anxious apprehensions are twisted together in the threads that connect the parent with the child!"

—Samuel Griswold Goodrich

I Love You
You
Dad
C O U P O N S

Dad, because I love you, I will make your lunch

Personal notes _____

_____

"*I can still look to the example my father set and get the sustenance I need.*"

—Tyne Daly

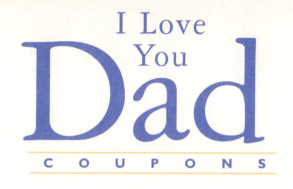

I Love You
You
Dad

C O U P O N S

Dad, because I love you, I won't have my friends over Saturday night

Personal notes _____

_____

"The best portion of a good man's life—
his little, nameless, unremembered acts
of kindness and of love."

—William Wordsworth

I Love You Dad

COUPONS

Dad, because I love you, I will refuse my allowance for a week

Personal notes _____

_____

"A wise son maketh a glad father."

—Proverbs 10:1

I Love You
Dad

C O U P O N S

THIS COUPON ENTITLES DAD TO TWO HOURS OF FREE TIME TO TINKER AROUND IN THE GARAGE, AT HIS WORKBENCH, ETC.

Personal notes _____

_____

"The family is one of nature's masterpieces."

—George Santayana

I Love You
You
Dad
C O U P O N S

DAD, BECAUSE I LOVE YOU, I WILL DO MY HOMEWORK WITHOUT BEING TOLD

Personal notes _____

_____

"A man cannot leave a better legacy to the world than a well-educated family."

—Thomas Scott

I Love
You
Dad

C O U P O N S

INSTANT COUPON!

Get off the phone!

Personal notes _____

_____

"*A man can do only what he can do. But if he does that each day he can sleep at night and do it again the next day.*"

—Albert Schweitzer

I Love You Dad

COUPONS

DAD, BECAUSE I LOVE YOU, I WILL GO TO YOUR OFFICE AND HELP YOU WITH ANYTHING YOU NEED HELP WITH FOR A DAY

Personal notes _____

_____

"No man can possibly know what life means, what the world means, what anything means, until he has a child and loves it. And then the whole universe changes and nothing will ever again seem exactly as it seemed before."

—Lafacadio Hearn

I Love You
Dad
C O U P O N S

This coupon
entitles Dad to
a day free of errands

Personal notes _____

_____

"*The one thing children wear out faster than shoes is parents.*"

—John J. Plomp

I Love
You
Dad

C O U P O N S

Dad, because I love you, I will *go* fishing with you

Personal notes _____

_____

"Like father, like son."

—Unknown

I Love
You
Dad

C O U P O N S

Turn off the TV!

Personal notes _____

_____

"Children have never been very good at listening to their elders, but they have never failed to imitate them."

—James Baldwin

I Love You Dad

COUPONS

DAD, BECAUSE I LOVE YOU, I WILL MAKE YOUR BED

Personal notes _____

_____

"I looked at that kid for a long time, I felt something impossible for me to explain in words…Then it came to me. I was a father."

—Nat "King" Cole

I Love
You
Dad
C O U P O N S

**Dad, because I
love you, I won't
play loud music
for a week**

Personal notes _____

_____

"*A wise son heeds his father's instruction.*"

—Proverbs 13:1

I Love
You
Dad

C O U P O N S

Dad, because
I love you, I won't
ask to borrow
money…today!

Personal notes _____

_____

"*A father is a banker provided by nature.*"

—French proverb

I Love
You
Dad

C O U P O N S

Personal notes _____

_____

THIS COUPON ENTITLES
DAD TO HIS CHOICE
OF RADIO STATIONS
IN THE CAR

"*No music is so pleasant to my ears as that word—father.*"

—Lydia Maria Child

I Love You
Dad

C O U P O N S

Personal notes _____

_____

Dad, because **I** love you, **I** will brush my teeth without reminding for a week

"The very words 'my father' always make me smile."

—Angela Carter

I Love
You
Dad

C O U P O N S

Do your
homework!

Personal notes _____

_____

"One father is more than a hundred schoolmasters."

—George Herbert

I Love You

You

Dad

C O U P O N S

Dad, because I love you, I will take one shower or bath without argument

Personal notes _____

_____

"You don't raise heroes; you raise sons.
And if you treat them like sons, they'll
turn out to be heroes, even if it's
just in your own eyes."

—Walter Schirra, Sr.

I Love You
You
Dad
C O U P O N S

Personal notes _____

DAD PICKS THE MOVIE.
THIS COUPON ENTITLES
DAD TO THE MOVIE OF
HIS CHOICE AT THE
VIDEO STORE

"*A father is a man who is always learning how to love. He knows that his love must grow and change because his children change.*"

—Tim Hansel

I Love
You
Dad

C O U P O N S

Personal notes _____

_____

DAD, BECAUSE I LOVE YOU, I WILL PUT MY TOYS AWAY TODAY

"*The righteous man walks in his integrity;*
His children are blessed after him."

—Proverbs 20:7

I Love You
You
Dad

C O U P O N S

Personal notes _____

_____

Pack the picnic basket,
and let's go for a hike!

"The world tips away when we look into our children's faces."

—Louise Erdrich

I Love You Dad

COUPONS

Dad, because I love you, I will not ask for the car keys Saturday night

Personal notes _____

_____

"The finest inheritance you can give to a child is to allow it to make its own way, completely on its own feet."

—Isadora Duncan

I Love
You
Dad
C O U P O N S

This coupon entitles Dad to one free foot massage

Personal notes _____

_____

"When you look at your life, the greatest happinesses are family happinesses."

—Dr. Joyce Brothers

I Love You
You
Dad
C O U P O N S

DAD, BECAUSE I LOVE
YOU, I WILL DO THE
DISHES

Personal notes _____

_____

"*The sound of his father's voice was a necessity. He longed for the sight of his stooped shoulders as he had never, in the sharpest of his hunger, longed for food.*"

—Marjorie Kinnan Rawlings

I Love You
Dad
You
C O U P O N S

CURFEW COUPON.
BE HOME BY _____

Personal notes _____
_____

"*Who holds the souls of children,
holds the nation.*"

—Unknown

I Love You
Dad
You
C O U P O N S

Dad, because I love you, I will clean my room for a week without being asked

Personal notes _____

_____

"It is the longing for the father that lives in each of us from his childhood days, for the same father whom the hero of legend boasts of having overcome."

—Sigmund Freud

I Love You Dad

C O U P O N S

This coupon is good for one week of sibling peace

Personal notes _____

_____

"*Blessed indeed is the man who hears many gentle voices call him father!*"

—Lydia M. Child

I Love You Dad

COUPONS

I Love My Pet Coupon.
Dad, because I love you,
I will: wash the dog, clean
the litterbox, walk the pet,

_____ (fill in the blank)

Personal notes _____

_____

"*Family life is the source of the greatest human happiness.*"

—Robert J. Gavighurst

I Love
You
Dad

C O U P O N S

DAD PICKS THE PIZZA.
THIS COUPON
ENTITLES DAD TO
PICK THE TOPPINGS
AND CRUST OF
HIS CHOICE

Personal notes _____

_____

"*Children reinvent your world for you.*"

—Susan Sarandon

I Love You
You
Dad
C O U P O N S

DAD, BECAUSE I LOVE YOU, I WILL CLEAN THE BATHROOM

Personal notes _____

_____

"*A happy childhood is one of the best gifts that parents have it in their power to bestow.*"

—Mary Cholmondeley

I Love You
Dad
C O U P O N S

The "Dad can say no" Coupon. Don't ask, the answer is no!

Personal notes _____

_____

"It is a wise father that knows his own child."

—Shakespeare

I Love
You
Dad
C O U P O N S

Personal notes _____

_____

Friends go home!

"It is not possible for civilization to flow backwards while there is youth in the world."

—Helen Keller

I Love
You
Dad
C O U P O N S

This coupon entitles
Dad to one big hug

Personal notes _____

_____

"Directly after God in Heaven comes Papa."

—Wolfgang Amadeus Mozart

Send us your coupon idea!

What do you most want to give dad? Dads, what do you really want from your loved ones? Send us your coupon ideas—if we use them in our next book or in future editions, we'll send you a free copy of the finished book! Submission of ideas implies free and clear permission to use in any and all future editions. Send your coupons to:

Sourcebooks
Attn: Coupon Ideas
P.O. Box 372
Naperville, IL 60566

Other great coupon books from Sourcebooks

I Love You Mom Coupons
Golf Coupons
Love Coupons, by Gregory J.P. Godek, author of *1001 Ways to Be Romantic*
The Best of Friends Coupons
The Chocoholic's Coupon Book
Happy Birthday Coupons
My Favorite Teacher Coupons
Merry Christmas Coupons

These titles and other Sourcebooks publications are available now at your local book or gift store, or by calling Sourcebooks at (630) 961-3900.